A Kacvinsky Family Album

Memories of Moquah

A Kacvinsky Family Album

Memories of Moquah

by Gwendolyn Holbrow

A Kacvinsky Family Album
Memories of Moquah

ISBN-13: 978-0692598498

ISBN-10: 0692598499

Library of Congress Control Number: 2015920652

Printed in U.S.A

Cover photo by D. Young, Skypix, approximately 1980: Joe and Maryann Kacvinsky's farm, County G, Moquah, with Steven and Mary Kacvinsky's farm in the background. Jim's maroon Mercedes can be seen behind the trees, by the barn. The cows belong to neighbor Ralph Mashlan.

Dedication

This little book is dedicated to the descendants of twin brothers Joseph John and John Joseph Kacvinsky.

It isn't meant to be a complete history, just a way to share a few photos and memories of the Kacvinsky family, which I joined when I married Mark Kacvinsky in 1981. Joe had already passed away in 1972, and Maryann followed him in 1990, so most of their grandchildren never knew them. We were fortunate to have Uncle Johnny and Auntie Eva with us a little longer. I hope the children and grandchildren and great-grandchildren of Mary Ann and Joe, and of Joe's twin brother Johnny and his wife Eva, will enjoy reminiscing over these snapshots of a time and place that now seems very far away. The photos are all the black and white ones we happen to have, perhaps a bit Mark-centered (for obvious reasons), and I welcome new information, stories and photographs from the rest of the family. Perhaps we will need a second edition, or a sequel in color!

With love from
Gwendolyn Holbrow

Joe

Joseph John and John Joseph Kacvinsky were born on March 4, 1921. According to family lore, their mother didn't know she was carrying twins. John Joseph was born first, but was so blue and still, the birth attendants discretely placed him in a box under the bed in order to spare Mary the grief of knowing about the baby who had died. Joseph John arrived safely and was settling in, when a weak cry from under the bed notified everyone present that they had made a big mistake! They retrieved Johnny from under the bed and he went on to survive and thrive.

This picture of the twins was taken with their sister Esther in an apple orchard in September of 1922.

This is the twin's mother, born Mary Elizabeth Mrofchak, hard at work on their farm in Moquah, Wisconsin. She had immigrated to the United States and worked as a "salad girl" in a hotel before her marriage. Steven Joseph Kacvinsky arrived on Ellis Island around 1904 (listed there as "The Stefan Kacvinsky Family"). The two met in Ironwood, Michigan, and married on January 20, 1908. They went on to have ten children, six boys and four girls. Mary once appeared on the television game show Queen For A Day.

That's Joe on the left and Johnny on the right; Joe would plan their troublemaking and Johnny would carry it out. They must have been a handful! This photo is from about 1930.

The children of Steven and Mary Kacvinsky: John, Joe, Henry, Steve, Mary, Tom and Paul, in the late 1930s. Not shown: Margaret, Esther and Helen.

Here are all the boys with their dad, Steven. Johnny and Joe both have stylish contrasting pocket flaps.

Joseph kacvinsky w/arrow
Bud Offman far left   Moqaah

Traditional and modern farm tractors.

Maryann

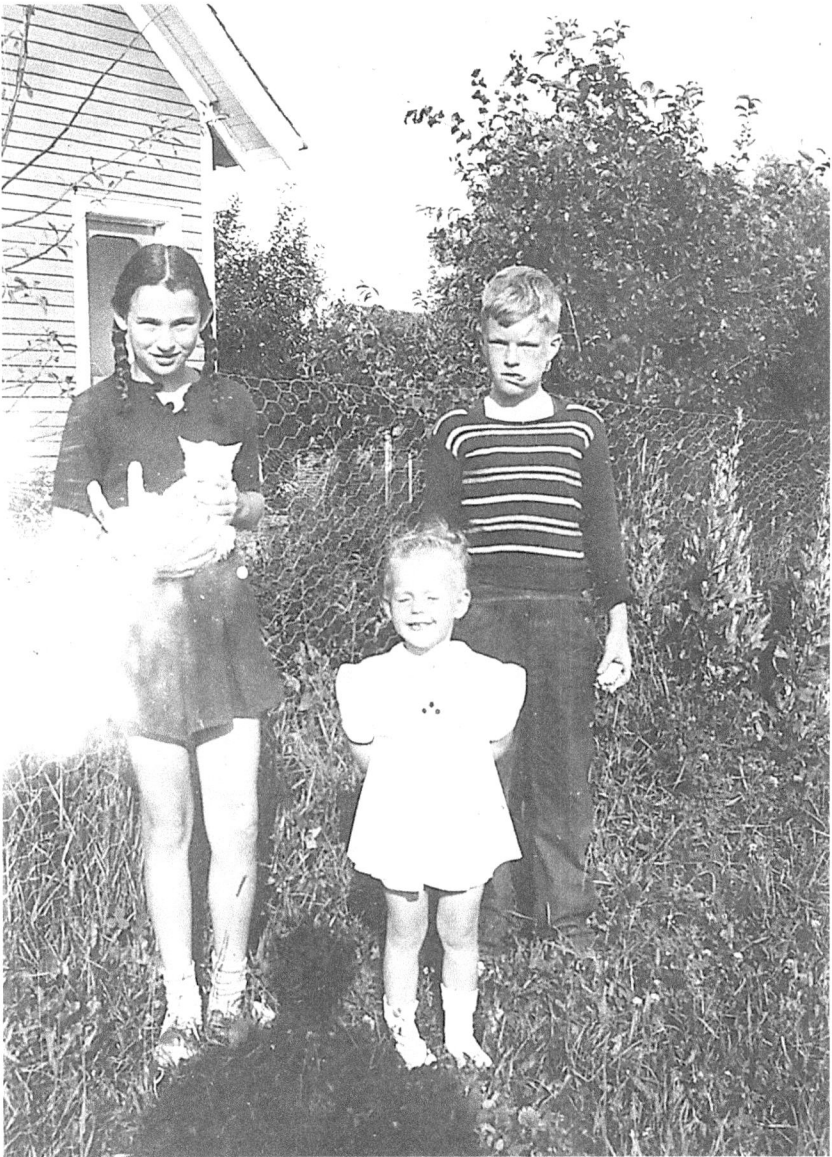

Here is Maryann in the spring of 1941, age 12, holding the cat, with her brother Tom and Mary Lloyd Love. Mary Lloyd was the daughter of the Kacvinsky twins' older sister Mary and her husband Lloyd Love.

Maryann

Tom

Mary Lloyd

Maryann's birth certificate calls her Mary Ann Whitaker Mathews, and says she was born to Henry T. Mathews and Jeannette Margaret Whitaker in Chicago on March 31, 1929. She was later to learn that she had in fact been left at The Cradle Society as an infant and was adopted. Despite repeated attempts, she was never able to discover her birth parents; she learned only that one was Irish and one was German, and that they were Roman Catholics in good health.

Maryann's father, known as Tom, was born in Ashland, WI, and was a hard drinking, bad-tempered Chicago stockbroker. After adopting Maryann, he and Jeanette went on to have three more children, Henry T. Mathews, Jr., Michael, and Jeannette.

When Maryann was only ten, her mother died. The family remained connected to Ashland, visiting relatives there every summer, and on July 16, 1942, Tom married Margaret Elizabeth Kacvinsky of nearby Moquah. She was the Kacvinsky twins' older sister, aka Aunt Margaret to their future children. This is probably a photo of her. She and Tom had two more children, Patrick and Timothy.

Marylou - Tom
Jeanette Mathews
Patrick

The family lived in Evanston, Illinois, and they were well off; it looks as though they took a pretty nice vacation in the winter of 1946.

Maryann Mathews, age 17

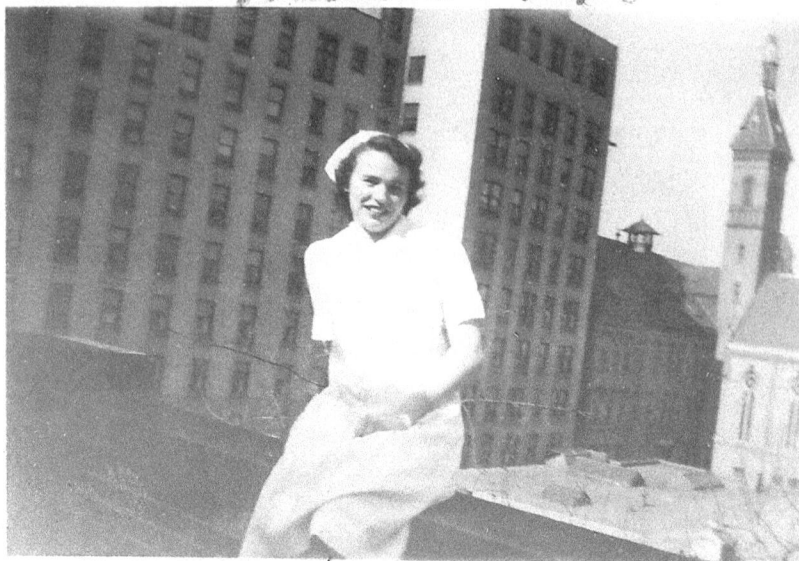

Nursis training
March 1948

Maryann graduated from nursing school in 1948. She is on
the right below, with a nursing school friend on the left.

Mary Ann Mathews   June 1948

Joe and Maryann's Wedding

May 26, 1951

Back: Rudy Misun, Steve Lajcak, Joseph Kacvinsky, Maryann Mathews Kacvinsky, Jeanette Mathews (Maryann's sister), Barbara Mathews (Maryann's cousin)

Front: Patrick Mathews (Maryann's brother), Diane Kacvinsky (daughter of Joe's twin brother John)

Maryann's cousin Barbara, between the windows, is enjoying the wedding breakfast! Cousin Diane, far left, was flower girl; Johnny had married Auntie Eva and begun a family years before Maryann finally persuaded Joe to settle down. The twins' parents, Mary and Steve, sit with their backs to us in the right foreground. Aunt Margaret is in the back corner, under the lamp, wearing a wide stylish hat. Since she was Joe's sister and married Maryann's father, she was now both stepmother and sister-in-law to Maryann, and became both aunt and grandmother to their children. She and Maryann did not get along particularly well and in later years would have some extremely heated philosophical discussions about child-rearing!

Mathews - Kacvinsky

By Special Correspondent.

MOQUAH — Before an all white setting of gladioli and candalbra in the chancel of S. S. Peter and Paul's Church, Saturday, May 26th. Mary Ann Mathews, daughter of Mr. and Mrs. Henry Mathews of Evanston, Ill. became the bride of Joseph Kacvinsky, son of Mr. and Mrs. Steve Kacvinsky of Moquah in a double ring ceremony. The Rev. Fr. Florian Herides officiated at the 10 o'clock Nuptial Mass.

Preceding the arrival of the wedding party, Miss Connie Moravetz sang beautiful hymns to the Blessed Virgin accompanied by Mrs. Mary Guerrera at the organ.

As the wedding march from "Lohengrin" was played the bride walked down the aisle on the arm of her father, who gave her in marriage, followed by her attendants. The choir sang the choral Mass by W. J. Marsh. During the Offertory, Miss Moravetz rendered Gounod's "Ave Maria" and at Communion, "Oh Lord I Am Not Worthy." For the Recessional, Miss Moravetz sang, "On This Day, O Beautiful Mother," accompanied by Mrs. Guerrera at the organ.

For her wedding day, the bride chose a lovely gown of white lace and net. The tight fitting bodice had the traditional long pointed sleeves and the bouffant skirt fell into a long graceful train. Her fingertip veil of net was gathered to a Juliet cap. She carried a bouquet of white June roses.

Miss Jeanette Mathews of Evanston, sister of the bride was maid of honor. Her gown was of ice blue lace, with fitted bodice and ballerina length skirt. She wore a matching Juliet cap and carried a bouquet of peach gladioli.

A cousin of the bride, Miss Barbara Mathews of Ashland served as bridesmaid. She wore a gown of dusty rose net, with fitted bodice and ballerina length skirt. Her Juliet cap matched her gown and she also carried a bouquet of peach gladioli.

Diane Kacvinsky, niece of the groom, made a pretty flower girl in her all white dress of organdy and lace. Her bouquet was a puff of net with tiny flowers, tied with a blue ribbon, that matched the one in her hair. Ring bearer was Patrick Mathews of Evanston, brother of the bride.

Attending the groom was Steve Lajcak as best man and Rudy Misun as usher.

Following the ceremony a wedding breakfast was served at the Menard Hotel for the immediate families.

A reception was held at the Moquah school house in the evening where about four hundred guests greeted the newlyweds. Dinner was served followed by a wedding dance.

First comes love, then comes marriage, then comes...
Joey, born in September of 1952

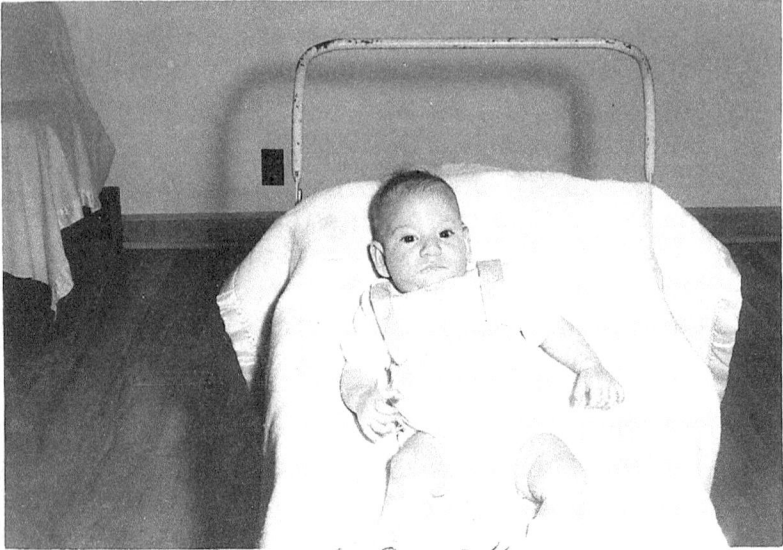

Joseph Jr. 2½ mo.

Building the House

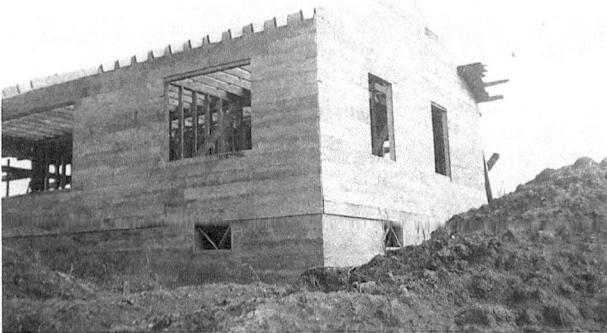

It wasn't long until they needed to build an addition!

A Growing Family

Joe with Joey and Peggy on the front steps of the new house.

Peggy and Joey

Joey in the wading pool.

Joey, Tommy and Peggy, Christmas 1955

Peggy watching Daddy shave.

January 1957

Cousin Joanne, Cousin Stevie, Joey, Cousin Susie, Peggy, Cousin Diane holding Tommy. The cousins are all the children of Joe's twin brother, aka Uncle Johnny, and Auntie Eva.

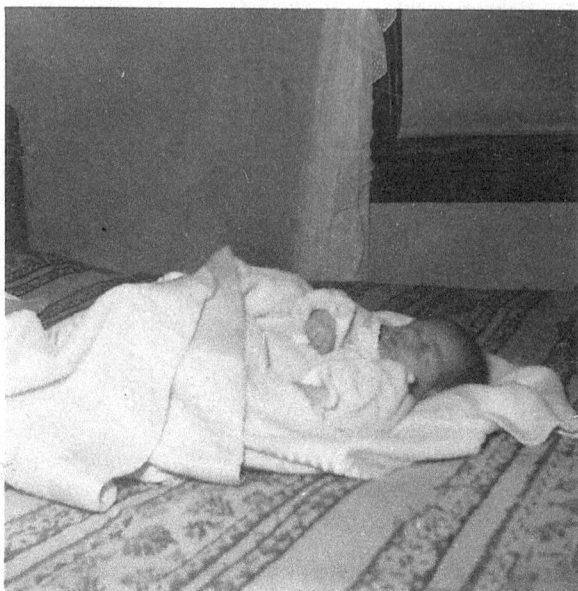

Mark -
Christmas 1958

Spotty, probably winter of 1958-59

Markie
6 1/2 months

Nov. 1959

Mark in the playpen, Joe at left

Jan 1959

Mark
Beth
Peggy
Tommy
Joey

Nov. 1959

Mark and Joey on the floor, Joe on the couch.

Dec. 1959

Back: Mark and Cousin Stevie
Middle: Joey, Cousin Billy, Beth, Cousin Susie, Peggy
Front: Tommy

Merry Christmas, 1959, from
Beth, Joey, Markie, Peggy, and Tommy.

Back: Cousin Joanne holding Beth, Cousin Susie, Cousin Diana holding Cousin Billy and Tommy. Front: Peggy, Cousin Stevie, Joey

The calendar on the wall says December 1960.

Joey, Beth, Peggy, Tommy

Mary Jo
Monk

March 1964

Tommy, Mark and Spotty

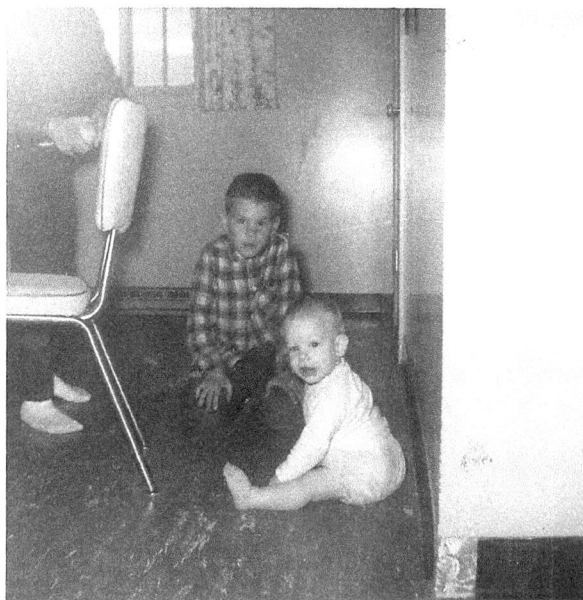

Mark and Jimmy, 1964

Mark, Mary Jo & Jimmy
March 1964

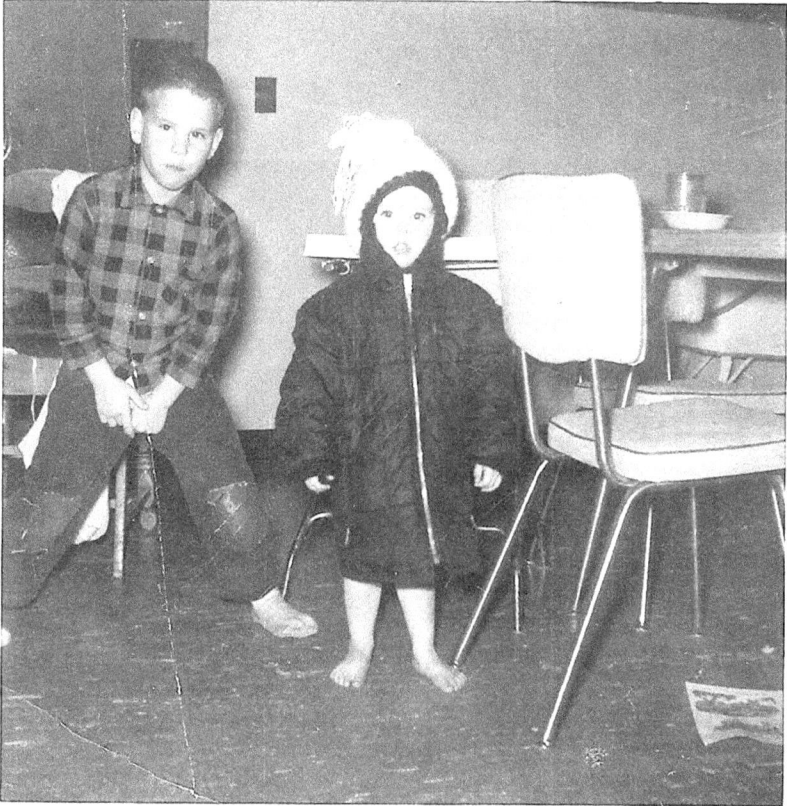

Mark and Mary Jo, 1964

Mary Jo, Mark and Peggy, Easter 1964

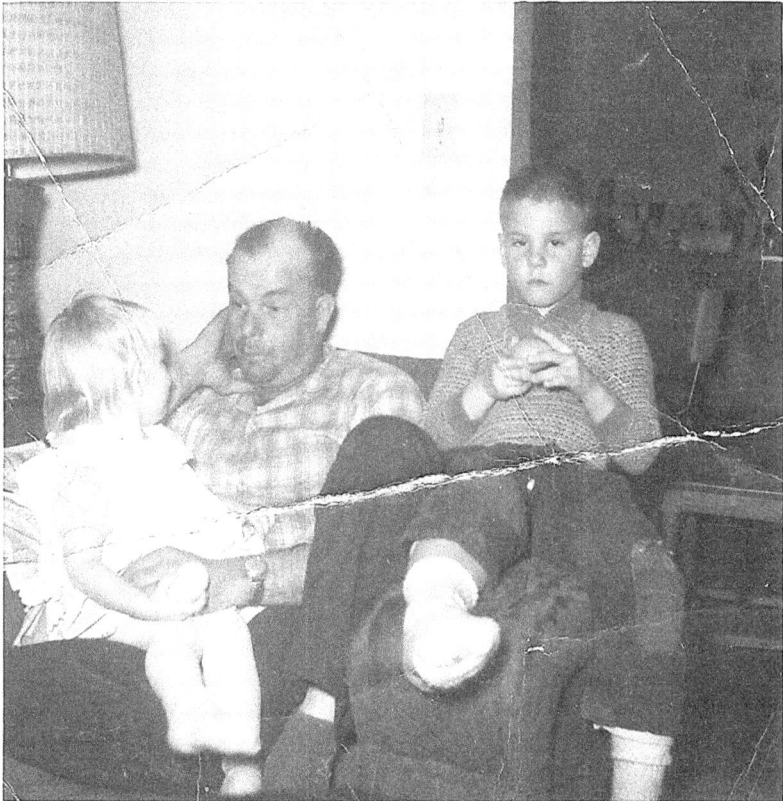

Mary Jo, Joe and Mark, 1964

2015

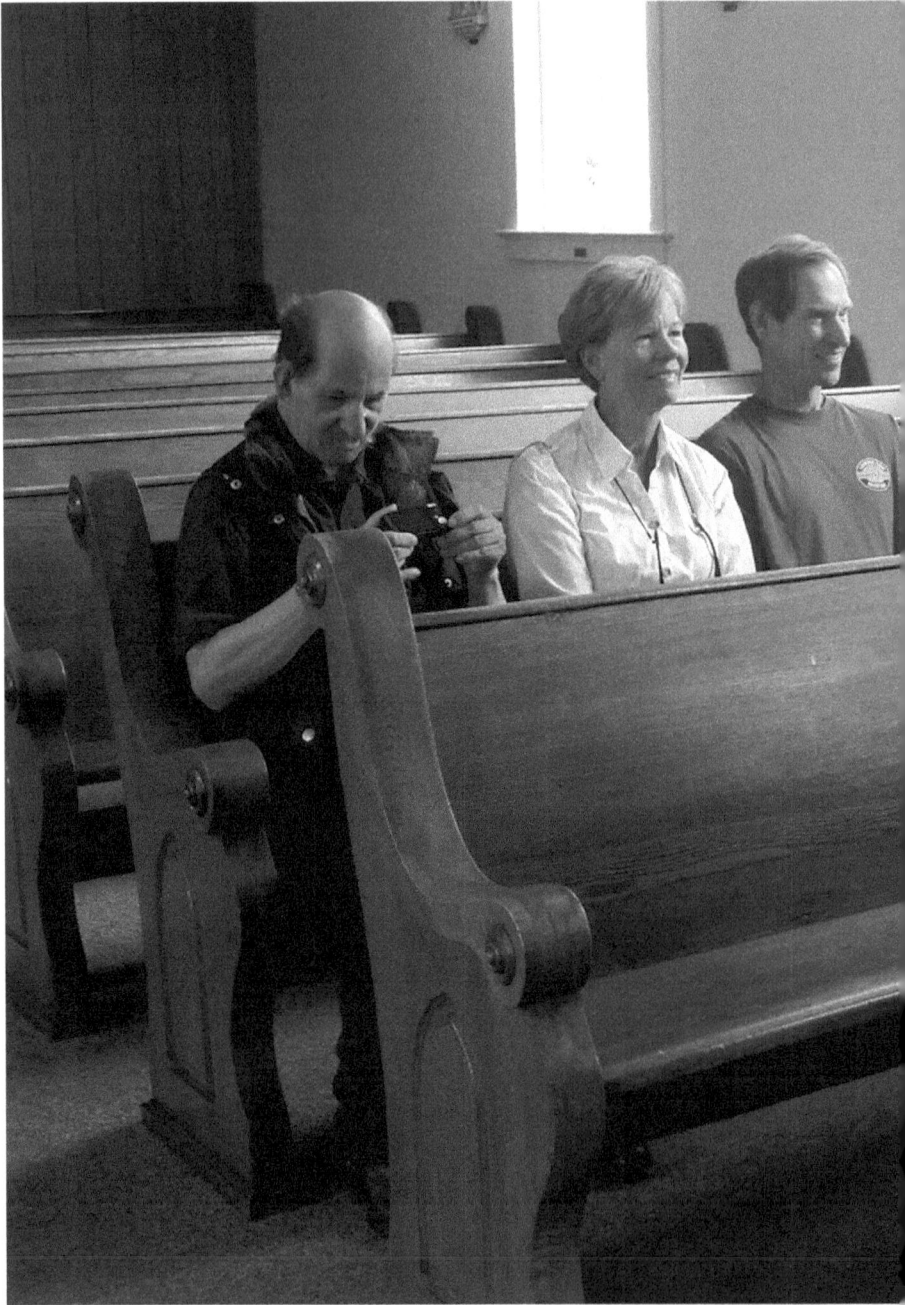

August 2015

Reunion at the Moquah church, Saints Peter and Paul, of all
the children of Joe and Maryann.

Left to right: Joe Kacvinsky, Peggy Good, Tom Kacvinsky,
Beth Kacvinsky, Mark Holbrow, Mary Jo Kacvinsky, Jim Kacvinsky

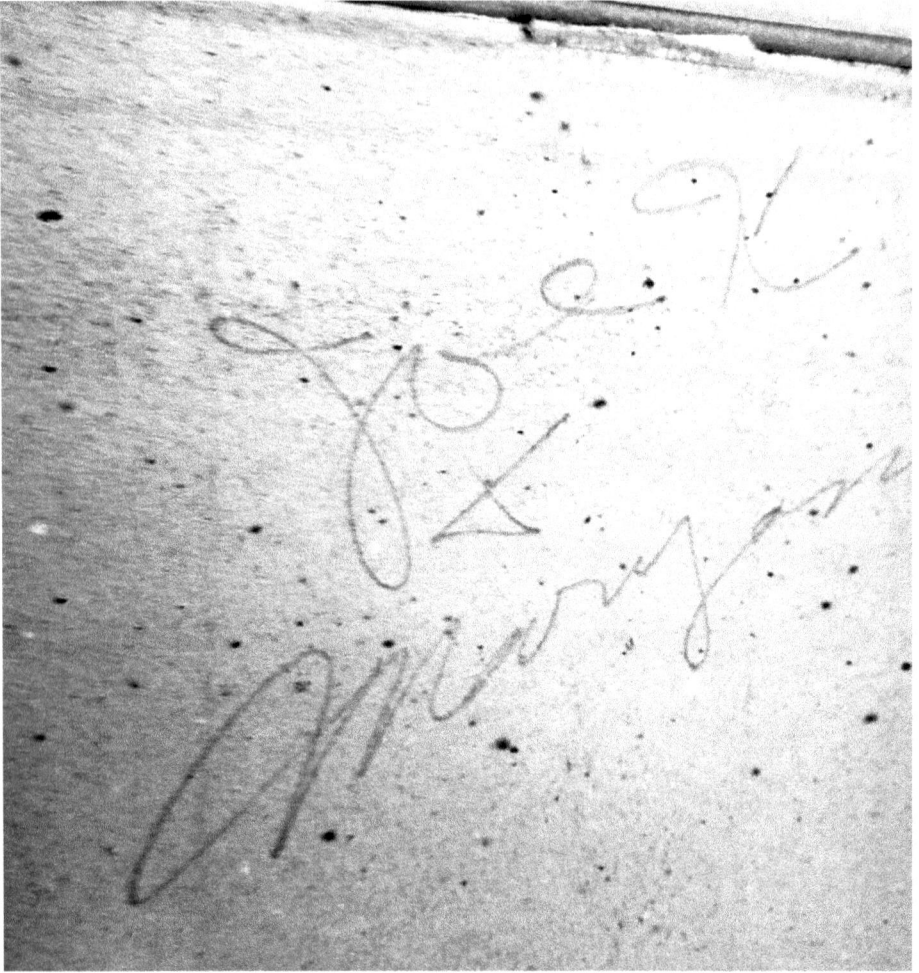

September 2015

The current owner of the house that Joe built hired Bob
Sell to replace some sheetrock. When Bob opened up the
wall, he found these words written inside it:

"Joe K. + Maryann"

Photo credits

Photos from the 1950s and 60s were taken by Maryann Kacvinsky, D. Young of Skypix took the aerial cover photo, Bob Sell took the photo of the writing on the wall, and Gwendolyn Holbrow took the contemporary photo of the Kacvinsky siblings in the Moquah church. Charles H. Holbrow took the author photo. Origins of the others are veiled in the mists of time.

www.ingramcontent.com/pod-product-compliance
Lightning Source LLC
Chambersburg PA
CBHW060658030426
42337CB00017B/2674